WILDLIFE AT RISK

# ENDANGERED
# ORANGUTANS

Jane Katirgis and Lisa Harkrader

**Enslow Publishing**

101 W. 23rd Street
Suite 240
New York, NY 10011
USA

enslow.com

Published in 2016 by Enslow Publishing, LLC.
101 W. 23rd Street, Suite 240, New York, NY 10011

**Library of Congress Cataloging-in-Publication Data**

Katirgis, Jane, author.
 Endangered orangutans / Jane Katirgis and Lisa Harkrader.
     pages cm. — (Wildlife at risk)
 Summary: "Discusses orangutans, why they are endangered and how they are being helped"—Provided by publisher.
 Audience: Ages 11+.
 Audience: Grades 7 to 8.
 Includes bibliographical references and index.
 ISBN 978-0-7660-6886-5 (library binding)
 ISBN 978-0-7660-6884-1 (pbk.)
 ISBN 978-0-7660-6885-8 (6-pack)
 1.  Orangutans—Juvenile literature. 2.  Endangered species—Juvenile literature. 3.  Orangutans—Conservation—Juvenile literature.  I. Harkrader, Lisa, author. II. Title.
 QL737.P94K38 2016
 599.88'3—dc23

                              2015009974

Printed in the United States of America

**To Our Readers:** We have done our best to make sure all Web site addresses in this book were active and appropriate when we went to press. However, the author and the publisher have no control over and assume no liability for the material available on those Web sites or on any Web sites they may link to. Any comments or suggestions can be sent by e-mail to customerservice@enslow.com.

Portions of this book originally appeared in the book *The Orangutan*.

**Photos Credits:** Anup Shah/Stone/Getty Images, p. 7; Christopher Chan/Moment/Getty Images, p. 1 (orangutans); Creativ Studio Heinemann/Creative (RF)/Getty Images, p. 1 (borage flowers); Dirk Freder/Vetta/Getty images, p. 16; hudiemm/E+/Getty Images (notebook fact boxes throughout book); Joakim Leroy/E+/Getty Images, p. 1 (palm leaf); Jonas Gratzer/LightRocket via Getty Images, p. 33; Louise Murray/Robert Harding World imagery/Getty Images, p. 43; Maria Toutoudaki/Photodisk/Getty Images (background paper texture throughout book); Maurice Lee Choong Min/E+/Getty images, p. 14; ODD ANDERSEN/AFP/Getty Images, p. 39; Paula Bronstein/Getty Images North America/Getty Images, pp. 37, 41; Paul & Paveena McKenzie/Oxford Scientific/Getty Images, p. 23; Rodney Brindamour/National Geographic/Getty Images, p. 27; seng chye teo/Moment/Getty Images, p. 11; shenzhen harbour/Moment/Getty Images, p. 32.

**Cover Credits:** Christopher Chan/Moment/Getty Images (orangutans); Creativ Studio Heinemann/Creative (RF)/Getty Images (borage flowers); Joakim Leroy/E+/Getty Images (palm leaf); Maria Toutoudaki/Photodisk/Getty Images (background paper texture).

# CONTENTS

# Orangutans at a Glance

## Scientific Name

Sumatran orangutans are *Pongo abelii*.
Bornean orangutans are *Pongo pygmaeus*.

## Height

Males average 4.5 feet (1.35 meters).
Females average 3.5 feet (1.05 meters).

## Weight

Males weigh from 165 to 300 pounds (75 to 136 kilograms) in the wild and up to 400 pounds (180 kilograms) or more in captivity.
Females weigh from 80 to 120 pounds (36 to 54 kilograms).

## Hair

Shaggy reddish brown to light orange.
The hair of Bornean orangutans is smoother and browner.
The hair of Sumatran orangutans is fluffier and redder.

## Range

The rain forests of Borneo and Sumatra, two islands located in Southeast Asia.

## Breeding Season

None. Orangutans, like humans, can breed at any time throughout the year, but females only mate and give birth every 3 to 5 years.

## Gestation

8.5 months

## Number of Young in One Birth

Usually only one

## Life Span

Up to 60 years in captivity

## Status

Bornean orangutans are endangered. Sumatran orangutans are critically endangered.

## Number of Individuals Remaining

Approximately 45,000–69,000 in Borneo and 7,300 in Sumatra

## Main Threat to Survival

Humans, who clear thousands of acres of rain forest each year for agriculture, logging, and mining.

# chapter one
# GREAT APES OF ASIA

They are the largest tree-dwelling animals in the world. They are red apes that have long fascinated explorers. They are two distinct species—Sumatran and Bornean—and they are both endangered. They are orangutans, the only great apes of Asia.

Some native people of Borneo and Sumatra believed these apes were God's first try at making humans. Others thought they were humans who had fled to the forest. Many native people believed these creatures knew how to talk but refused to speak in front of humans because they were afraid humans would put them to work.

## Numbers Are Dropping

In ancient times, orangutans ranged through Southeast Asia into Southern China and as far west as India. But at the end of the last ice age, ten thousand to twenty thousand years ago, orangutans disappeared on the mainland of Asia. Today they survive only in small pockets of rain forest on the islands of Sumatra and Borneo. Sumatra is part of the country of Indonesia. Borneo, the third largest island in the world after Greenland and Papua New

A mother and baby orangutan, two examples of the endangered red apes, live in a reserve in Borneo, Indonesia.

Guinea, is divided into three countries. The Southeastern two thirds of the island is part of Indonesia. The northern third is part of Malaysia. The tiny independent country of Brunei is notched out of the Northwestern coast. Orangutans live in the Indonesian and Malaysian parts of Borneo.

Scientists estimate that in 1900, there were more than three hundred thousand orangutans living in the wild. Today, between 45,000 and 59,000 live in Borneo, while about 7,300 live in Sumatra.[1]

Bornean orangutans are listed as endangered, and Sumatran orangutans are critically endangered. Many countries give orangutans legal protection as endangered species. But their population has shrunk by half since the 1950s. The biggest threat to orangutans is the loss of their habitat. Eighty percent of Indonesia's original rain forests have been cleared for logging, farming, and mining. The habitat loss continues; each year, more than 6 million acres (2.4 million hectares) are destroyed.[2] Many scientists predict that without major conservation efforts, orangutans could become extinct by 2035.

## No Pets Allowed

In the 1980s, a popular television program called *The Naughty Family* aired in Taiwan. The show starred a family that owned a pet orangutan. Since then, many people in Asia have clamored to own pet orangutans, and although it is against the law to sell orangutans because they are endangered, an illegal orangutan trade has sprung up. Poachers kill mother orangutans and take their babies to sell as

pets on the black market. About two thirds of the captured babies die.

Researchers estimate that two hundred to five hundred baby orangutans are traded each year as pets. About twice that many die on their way to be sold, and poachers also kill the mother orangutans to capture their babies.

Those surviving babies do not fare well. Baby orangutans are cute and cuddly, but those babies grow up. Adult orangutans weigh as much as or more than adult humans and are much stronger. They are hard to manage, which leads some owners to abandon them. Others take them to rehabilitation centers, where experts work toward one day releasing them into the wild.

## Conservation Challenges

Wild orangutans do not live in one country. Part of their habitat is in Indonesia, and part is in Malaysia. The borders between the countries make it hard to coordinate conservation efforts. The rain forest habitat is dense and remote, which makes it difficult for

## Fast Fact!

When it rains, orangutans make umbrellas out of large leaves.

governments to enforce conservation laws and keep orangutans and their habitat safe.

In recent years, the Indonesian government went through a state of upheaval. The political unrest made orangutan protection even more difficult. And the horrible destruction and loss of life in coastal Sumatra caused by the earthquake and tsunami of December 2004 made it more difficult to save orangutans in a place where many people had little to begin with.

The poverty of this region is also one of the reasons that poaching goes on. Since those who sell endangered animals, such as orangutans, are often poor, they can make more money in less time in illegal trade than they can earn honestly over a longer period. Most conservationists point out that it is too easy to simply blame native peoples for the reduction in animal populations in their countries. Those who provide the demand for the animals themselves, as well as for the products that come from their habitats (such as tropical hardwoods), are at least as much to blame.

Finally, orangutans do not reproduce quickly. In fact, they reproduce more slowly than any other mammal. Female orangutans do not begin having babies until they are about twelve years old. They then give birth about every eight years and have only one baby at a time. A female orangutan will only have two to four babies in her lifetime. This slow reproduction rate means that when the orangutan population suffers a serious decline, it cannot bounce back quickly.

Because orangutans have only one baby about every eight years, it takes a long time to increase their population.

# chapter two

# MEET THE ORANGUTAN

Orangutans currently live in Borneo and Sumatra. The Bornean orangutan is one species, *Pongo pygmaeus,* and the Sumatran orangutan is *Pongo abelii.* Sumatran orangutans have closer social ties than the Bornean orangutans. The Sumatran apes have longer hair on their face. The Bornean orangutans come down to the ground more often.

The people of Borneo and Sumatra speak Malay. The orangutan's common name comes from two Malay words: *orang,* which means "person," and *hutan,* which means "forest." Orangutan, then, means "person of the forest." It is considered inappropriate in Southeast Asia, however, to refer to orangutans by the shortened form, *orang,* because of the word's meaning.

## Man's Closest Relatives

Orangutans, gorillas, chimpanzees, and bonobos (once called pygmy chimpanzees) all belong to a group known as the great apes. Great apes are man's closest relatives. In fact, some scientists think humans should be classified as great apes. By studying fossils and

DNA, scientists have determined that humans and apes evolved from a common ancestor that lived more than 15 million years ago. Chimpanzees and bonobos are the most genetically similar to us. They share nearly 99 percent of their genes with humans, and humans can receive blood transfusions from chimpanzees. Humans and orangutans share 98 percent of their genes.[1]

But humans and orangutans share some characteristics that chimpanzees and gorillas do not share. Humans and orangutans have more parasites in common. They both have a certain vein in their arms that other apes do not have.

All great apes can stand and walk upright, similar to the way humans walk, but orangutans more often travel on all fours. When bonobos, chimpanzees, and gorillas travel on all fours, they knuckle walk by leaning on the knuckles of their hands. By contrast, orangutans ball their fingers into fists when they walk on all fours.

## Life in the Canopy

Orangutans are covered with reddish brown hair, which gives them the nickname red apes. They have short legs and long arms that span 7 to 8 feet (2.1 to 2.4 meters) from fingertip to fingertip in the largest males. Their arms are almost as long as the length of their bodies and legs put together.

Orangutans are the world's largest arboreal, or tree-dwelling, animals, and their bodies are well suited to their treetop habitat. Their long fingers wrap around vines and branches in a powerful hooklike grip. Their thumbs are located low on their hands and far below their fingers. This helps keep an orangutan's thumbs out of the way when the animal brachiates, or moves hand over hand, as it travels from branch to branch.

Orangutans' handlike feet and rotating hip joints make them seem to have four arms instead of two arms and two legs. Any one of their limbs is strong enough to support their weight, so they can hang by one hand or one foot without falling. Their long arms and agile legs also help them reach fruit and other food. They can even eat with their feet!

This baby orangutan demonstrates how its arms and legs help it handle life in the trees.

## Female and Male Differences

Adult male orangutans are so different in appearance from adult female orangutans that it is easy to tell them apart just by looking at them. Because of these differences, scientists once considered them to be two separate species.

Wild adult male orangutans are 4 to 5 feet (1.2 to 1.5 meters) tall and weigh from 165 pounds to a hefty 300 pounds (75 to 136 kilograms). Female orangutans are about half that size. Adult females average 3.5 feet (1.05 meters) in height and weigh from 80 to 120 pounds (36 to 54 kilograms).

But the size difference is not the only thing that sets males and females apart. When males reach maturity at about age fifteen, they develop huge cheek pads that flare from the sides of their faces. These cheek pads make them look bigger and help them attract females. It is also believed that the cheek pads help the male's booming call travel farther in the forest to reach other orangutans in the widely spaced community. When male orangutans fight, they often bite each other's cheek pads.

Mature males also develop a large throat pouch. The pouch is an air sac that hangs down below the orangutan's chin. The male

## Fast Fact!

Of all the great apes, orangutans are the most solitary.

Huge cheek pads and a large throat pouch are two distinguishing features of an adult male orangutan.

uses his throat pouch to make his long call, a series of throaty grunts and roars that can be heard for more than half a mile. The long call attracts females and helps the male compete with other males.

## The Question of Subspecies

For many years, biologists divided orangutans into two subspecies. Orangutans that live in Borneo were known as *Pongo pygmaeus pygmaeus*. Orangutans from Sumatra were *Pongo pygmaeus abelii*.

Bornean orangutans and Sumatran orangutans look very similar, although they do have a few differences. Sumatran orangutans have longer, fluffier, redder hair. Bornean orangutans' hair tends to be thicker, smoother, darker, and browner. Bornean orangutans also have wider faces, and the cheek pads of Bornean males grow forward, which gives them a concave or dish-faced look.

In the 1980s, some scientists began questioning whether Sumatran and Bornean orangutans were more than subspecies. They believed the two groups could be separate species altogether. Borneo's orangutans live in five isolated populations, some of which are separated by mountain ranges. Researchers wondered if these populations were different enough to be considered separate subspecies.

In the 1990s, a team of scientists led by Dr. Stephen J. O'Brien compared the DNA of Sumatran and Bornean orangutans. They found that the two groups of orangutans are as genetically different from each other as lions are from tigers or horses from donkeys. In the great ape family, the orangutans are as different from each

## Fast Fact!
An adult male's call can be heard up to 0.6 miles (1 km) away.

other as common chimpanzees are from bonobos.[2] Chimpanzees and bonobos have long been recognized as separate species.

By studying the orangutans' DNA, Dr. O'Brien and his team determined that Sumatran and Bornean orangutans evolved from a common orangutan ancestor about one million to three million years ago.[3] They also discovered that the different populations of Bornean orangutans show very little genetic difference. They believe that until very recently these populations were not as separate as they are now. The populations only became isolated from each other within the last century as humans began clearing large areas of rain forest.[4]

chapter three

# Quiet Apes of the Forest

Orangutans live high in the treetops. They spend much of their day looking for fruit among the leaves. They have an important part in spreading the seeds of these fruits, too, so they are sometimes called the gardeners of the forest. Because orangutans live so high in the canopy and blend in with their surroundings, they are difficult to study in the wild.

## Getting Around

Orangutans do not move quickly, but they are experts at traveling among branches and vines. Wild female orangutans rarely set foot on the ground, even to find food or water. Adult males, though, do spend a fair amount of time on the ground, since they are usually too heavy to stay in the narrow tree branches. They eat fruits, plants, and animals they can find or catch in the trees. They drink rainwater that collects in the leaves and hollows of trees.

Orangutans are capable of walking. They sometimes walk on two feet, as humans do. But like other great apes, orangutans more often walk on all fours. They do not have the tough pads on their knuckles that gorillas and chimpanzees have. Instead, orangutans walk on the sides of their cupped hands and feet. Their walk looks a little awkward. Orangutans are much more confident and graceful when climbing and swinging through the trees.

## Family Dynamics

Adult orangutans are usually described as solitary apes, although they demonstrate the same levels of social abilities as the African apes. Adult male orangutans are certainly loners. They live alone and will not tolerate other adult males in their territory. They seek out female orangutans when it is time to mate. They stay with a female only for a short time and then move on. In Sumatra, male orangutans sometimes stay with females until the female gives birth. Scientists believe that Sumatran males may stay longer to protect the female from Sumatran tigers. Tigers do not live in Borneo.

Adult female orangutans are seldom alone. They do not live in the company of other adult orangutans, but they are almost always raising young. Female orangutans give birth to their first baby when they are about twelve years old. They raise the baby for eight or nine years. The young orangutan often stays close to its mother for the next two or three years as the female gives birth again and begins raising her next infant.

Although orangutans are semisolitary, they are also adaptable. In places where fruit is ripe and plentiful, several female orangutans will feed together in the same tree. In some swampy, remote areas of rain forest, orangutans live closer together and are more social.

Many orangutans, when freed from the constraints of their habitats, show a preference for social interaction with other orangutans.

## Traveling for Food

Adult orangutans establish home ranges. These are areas of the rain forest the orangutan travels through while gathering food. An orangutan's home range is not rigidly defined. Orangutans will venture beyond their usual ranges to find food. An orangutan's home range can stretch out over three square miles (eight square kilometers). In areas of rain forest where fruit and other food are abundant, ranges are smaller. In areas where food is scarce, ranges must be larger. A range must contain enough food to keep the orangutan alive.

## Meal Time

Orangutans are omnivores, eating both plants and animals. They eat leaves, nuts, shoots, honey, insects, and occasionally small birds and animals. In fact, the orangutan's diet is one of the most varied in the animal kingdom. Orangutans eat more than four hundred different kinds of food.

## Fast Fact!

Orangutans start their day with a two- to three-hour breakfast.

But orangutans are also called frugivores, or fruit eaters, because their favorite food, by far, is fruit. They love some of the same fruits we enjoy, such as figs and mangoes. One of their favorite fruits is the durian, a pungent fruit with a firm, prickly covering. The durian is popular with many animals in the rain forest, but its skin is so hard that other animals cannot eat it until the fruit is so ripe it bursts open. The strong and nimble-fingered orangutans, however, use their mouths and hands to open the fruit. Orangutans feast on durian long before other rain forest animals are able.

Orangutans are diurnal—active and awake during the day. Each night, adult orangutans build a nest of branches and leaves to sleep in, and they rarely use a nest more than once. They build the nests in trees 15 to 100 feet (4.6 to 30.5 meters) above the ground. Babies and young orangutans sleep in their mothers' nests.

## Life Cycle

Female orangutans give birth for the first time when they are about twelve years old. They are pregnant for about eight and a half months and usually give birth to one baby at a time.

Orangutan mothers give their new babies constant attention. For the first year, the orangutan mother carries her infant on her body all the time. The baby clings to its mother's hair and skin as she climbs through the forest.

At about age one, young orangutans become more independent. They stay very close to their mothers, but they no longer seem glued to her body. Their mothers teach them to climb, and the

The orangutan's favorite food is fruit. Animals that eat fruit are called frugivores.

babies begin exploring and learning to navigate branches and trees on their own.

Orangutans have a longer childhood than any other animal except humans. Young orangutans have a lot to learn and only one teacher. Their mothers teach them everything they need to know to survive in the rain forest. Mothers teach their young orangutans where to find the four hundred kinds of food that orangutans eat. At first, the mother orangutan feeds her baby bits of food she has already chewed. As the young orangutan grows, it begins gathering food on its own. Mothers also teach their babies how to find and open fruit when it is ripe and how to build nests and stay out of danger.

By the time an orangutan is six years old, she has begun venturing farther from her mother. No longer sleeping with her mother, she builds her own sleeping nest nearby. The mother orangutan will have her next baby when her first child is seven or eight years old. At first, the older orangutan child may stay close to the mother and new baby, but eventually she will go off to establish her own home range. Males tend to leave their mothers earlier and travel far away to establish their home ranges. Females stay with their mothers longer and establish ranges close by.

## Fast Fact!

When they are six months old, orangutans begin to practice building nests, and they are quite good at it by the time they are three years old.

chapter four

# How Smart Are Orangutans?

Imitation, or the ability to copy actions, is one skill that shows how intelligent orangutans are. They have been shown to copy humans in combing their hair, sawing wood, hammering nails, and even making a hammock. Planning, tool use, and language are other traits that show how orangutans and other great apes are highly intelligent species.

## Intelligence

Orangutans move slowly and deliberately. They often act as if they are not paying attention. For these reasons, people used to think orangutans were the least intelligent of the great apes.

But researchers have found that orangutans are just as bright as other great apes. In fact, orangutans do better than gorillas and chimpanzees on some intelligence tests. This is because different ape species solve problems differently. When chimpanzees face a problem, such as trying to get food out of a closed box, they tend to dive in actively and noisily. They first try one thing, then another.

If they do not succeed within a few minutes, they may give up in frustration.

Jumping at a problem with great energy and activity but a short attention span is not an effective way to tackle problems in the rain forest. That is probably why orangutans tend to be more deliberate problem solvers. They may look as if they are not really paying attention, but they are, in fact, constantly watching their environment very closely. They usually do not look at things head-on but from the corners of their eyes. Researchers think that orangutans ponder a problem and possible solutions to it before they act. When they finally go toward the box of food, they often approach it with a specific plan for opening it. They work through their plan step by step until it succeeds.

## Use of Simple Tools

One way in which scientists measure the intelligence of an animal species is by its use of tools. Species that use simple tools, such as sticks or rocks, are considered more intelligent than species that do not. Species that make or modify their tools are considered the most intelligent of all.

All great ape species use tools. They use sticks to dig for food on the ground, such as termites. They use rocks to break open nuts and fruits. Orangutans also use sticks to scratch their backs and leafy branches to swat away insects. They use large leaves as natural umbrellas to shelter them from the sun and rain.

Orangutans also make or modify their tools. They chew leaves so the leaves will act as sponges and absorb water from tree hollows.

The orangutans then suck the water from the leaves. When vines are too thin for an orangutan to travel on, orangutans can tie two vines together to increase their strength.

Orangutans are clever at imitating human behavior and learning to use human tools. Orangutans that have observed humans using boats to cross rivers have then untied the boats and set off across the water themselves. Captive orangutans have earned a reputation as

An orangutan uses a stick as a tool to open a coconut. They also use sticks to get honey from beehives.

escape artists. They continually find new ways to escape from their enclosures, such as by using a screwdriver to take apart a door's hinges. A large male orangutan named Fu Manchu kept escaping from his enclosure at the Omaha Zoo. The orangutan keepers finally discovered that Fu Manchu was using a piece of wire to pick the lock. During the day he would hide the wire in his mouth between his lip and gum.[1]

## Communication and Sounds

Great apes do not have the vocal structures that are required to produce human language, although they can produce sounds similar to ours. But they do have the ability to learn and use language. Researchers have taught great apes to communicate with humans through sign language. At the Think Tank's Orangutan Language Project at the Smithsonian Institution's National Zoo in Washington DC, orangutans learn to communicate by using special computers. The computers enable them to use about seventy different abstract symbols for words.

In the late 1970s, Dr. Gary Shapiro began teaching orangutans sign language at Camp Leakey, an orangutan research station in

Borneo. At first, the orangutans did not seem to be interested in what he was showing them—they did not even seem to be paying attention at all. But when they began using the signs, Dr. Shapiro realized that they had been watching him all along.

Not only can orangutans and other great apes learn signs or symbols for different objects and actions, but they also use those signs correctly. They combine different signs into phrases, such as give banana. They sometimes combine different signs to indicate a new object they do not already have a sign for. Chantek, a male orangutan at Zoo Atlanta, knows more than one hundred fifty signs. But he did not have a sign for Christmas, so he created his own: Red Hat Day.[2]

## Orangutan Culture

We think of culture as something that only describes humans. Groups of people who live in different parts of the world develop different cultures. The native people of Borneo, for example, developed social customs that were different from those of native Africans or Europeans.

Wildlife researchers are finding that individual populations of great ape species also develop different cultures, or sets of learned behaviors. The orangutans learn the behavior from each other and then pass it down from generation to generation. For example, orangutans often make a kiss-squeak noise when they are annoyed. But different orangutan populations make the kiss-squeak in different ways. Some Bornean populations kiss-squeak against a leaf to make the sound louder.

Orangutans in one Bornean population snag ride. Snag riding is sort of an orangutan sport. The orangutan jumps onto a falling branch and rides it down through the rain forest. The orangutan catches itself on other branches or vines before the falling branch crashes to the rain forest floor. Orangutans in Sumatra, as well as those in other Bornean populations, do not snag ride as far as researchers know.

One population of orangutans in Kutai National Park in Eastern Borneo uses leaves as napkins. Some of the fruits they eat are particularly messy. They wipe the juice from their faces with leaf napkins. Even though other orangutan populations eat these same fruits, only the Kutai orangutans use leaves as napkins. A population of Sumatran orangutans on one side of a river uses sticks to open fruit and dig out the seeds. However, the population of orangutans on the other side of the river does not. Researchers have found that orangutans that live in the most social populations, such as those living in the dense and swampy rain forests in Sumatra, share the largest number of learned behaviors.

# Fast Fact!

Wild figs are one of the orangutan's favorite fruits.

chapter five

# A LOOK TO THE FUTURE

The loss of forest habitat in Indonesia has many scientists fearful that in twenty years the orangutan will be extinct. Rebuilding after the Indian Ocean earthquake and tsunami of 2004 required significant timber resources and put further strain on the forest system.

Loss of habitat is also a critical problem in Malaysia. Environmentalists estimate that 190 acres (77 hectares) of Malaysian rain forest is felled every hour. The government of Malaysia continues to build large dams, such as the Bakun Dam in Borneo, which flood the surrounding land and destroy thousands of acres of rain forest.

## Forest Logging

The key to saving the orangutan or any endangered species is to find a way for humans and animals to exist together without either population harming the other. Logging destroys much of the orangutan's habitat. The rain forests of Sumatra and Borneo are rich havens of tropical hardwood trees. The economies of

Logging in Indonesia is a big threat to the orangutan's habitat.

Indonesia and Malaysia are poor, and the lumber from these trees is very valuable. Logging companies make a lot of money exporting lumber to other countries, and the industry creates much-needed jobs for local people. In addition, government officials often own the logging rights to areas of forest. These officials make money by leasing these rights to logging companies. So even though the rain forest is quickly disappearing, logging continues. Much of the logging is done illegally.

Logging companies also build roads through the rain forest, which destroys even more trees. The building of these roads erodes the soil and disrupts the natural balance of sunlight and humidity in the rain forest, which puts plant and animal species that live there in peril. Roads also give poachers greater access into the dense rain forest, which makes it easier for them to kill mother orangutans and steal their babies. In addition, loggers hunt for most of their own food, depleting the forests of some of the orangutan's natural food sources. Sometimes they also hunt orangutans for food.

This man is being arrested for illegal logging in Sumatra.

# A Compromising Idea

The Indonesian government tries to promote selective logging. In this method, rather than wiping out acres of rain forest at a time, loggers cut single trees here and there throughout the rain forest. Selective logging leaves the surrounding trees intact.

This sounds like a reasonable compromise. But rain forests are fragile and complicated ecosystems. The soil in a rain forest contains few nutrients. Most of the forest's nutrients lie in its towering trees. The tallest trees provide the most food and shelter for rain forest species. The tallest trees are the very trees that orangutans depend on for survival.

But the tallest trees are also the most valuable in the hardwood market. They are the trees that lumber companies target with selective logging. Even when loggers plant new trees to replace felled trees, the rain forest suffers permanent damage. In a natural cycle, when a tree dies, it falls to the floor of the rain forest. As the tree rots, its nutrients sink back into the soil and provide nourishment for young trees that spring up in its place. But when loggers remove a tree, its nutrients are gone forever. Nothing remains to nourish new trees. If loggers cut too many trees, the forest floor dries out and puts the entire forest at greater risk of fire. Orangutan populations in these logged forests have been seen to shrink by more than half.

# Palm Oil

Malaysia and Indonesia depend on palm oil to help their economies. Agricultural companies clear huge tracts of rain forest, up to 120 acres (49 hectares), for each palm plantation. To clear this land, plantation owners sometimes simply burn the forest down. In Borneo and Sumatra, almost all the lowland forests, the orangutan's favorite habitat, have been cleared. Orangutans have been forced into the higher forests where food is not as plentiful. Fewer orangutans can survive in these higher forests.

Orangutans love to eat palm hearts, so they often invade plantations while foraging for food and damage the palm trees. When plantation owners cannot scare them away or keep them out with fences, they often kill the trespassing orangutans. Some plantation owners put a bounty on orangutans. They pay local people up to a week's wages for each orangutan they kill.

## Gold

Gold mining has destroyed huge swaths of rain forest in Borneo. Miners use large water pumps and power hoses to blast away soil and dig holes into the earth. They leave behind nothing but craters in the barren sand. Miners also use heavy metals, such as mercury, to separate gold from sand. The mercury washes into the soil and runs into nearby streams and rivers, which poisons the land and water for the animals and people who depend on it to survive.

## Fires in the Forest

Over the years, forest fires have devastated Borneo and Sumatra. In 1983, the Great Fire of Borneo burned vast areas of rain forest. In 1997, immense fires erupted in Borneo. Fires in Sumatra and other nearby islands broke out as well. Logging made the forests even more vulnerable to fire. Loggers leave behind dried wood debris, as well as patches of grassland that grow up where the trees used to be, and these patches burn rapidly. The fires raged for months and became the worst forest fire in history. Smoke choked the air and polluted the water. In the end, 25 percent of the rain forest in Borneo was destroyed.

Today, fires are still set to clear the land to plant palm oil and timber plantations.

## Working to Save Orangutans

The Convention on International Trade in Endangered Species of Wild Fauna and Flora (CITES) regulates international trade in endangered plants and animals. CITES lists orangutans in Appendix 1, its list of most-endangered species. The United States listed orangutans as an endangered species in 1970 and offered the species additional regulations and protections. Many countries, including Malaysia, Indonesia, and Taiwan, have passed laws to protect orangutans. But these laws are hard to enforce against illegal loggers, miners, and poachers who sell orangutan babies as pets. Malaysia and Indonesia have established wildlife preserves and national parks. Rangers in these parks do their best to protect orangutans and other species, but it is often hard to guard the dense jungles.

Wildlife organizations around the world are fighting to save the orangutan. The Sumatran Orangutan Society, based in Bali but with branches in other countries, is on the front lines of the battle to save the critically endangered Sumatran orangutan. Orangutan

A volunteer feeds orphaned orangutans some milk at the Tanjung Puting National Park in Borneo, Indonesia.

Foundation International, the Borneo (or Balikpapan) Orangutan Survival Foundation, the World Wildlife Fund, and the Nature Conservancy help manage Bornean and Sumatran rain forests and help park rangers deal with illegal loggers and poachers. These groups try to protect orangutans that have overrun farms and plantations. They urge plantation owners to capture orangutans and take them to an orangutan rehabilitation center rather than killing them. They also try to educate people about the dangers that orangutans face and the ways in which humans can help them.

Zoos have also played an important part in helping to save endangered orangutans and educating the public on the plight of these great apes since orangutans generally do quite well in captivity. There are fifty-five zoological institutions in North America that participate in the Orangutan Species Survival Plan. The Orangutan SSP has led to the births of baby orangutans in captivity while the number of orangutans in the wild continues to drop. Zoo Atlanta, with thirteen orangutans, has the largest population of orangutans in North America. There are about eight hundred orangutans in zoos worldwide.

## Captive Orangutans

In 1971, Dr. Biruté Galdikas set up Camp Leakey in the Tanjung Puting Wildlife Reserve (now a national park) in Southern Indonesian Borneo. She has studied orangutans at Camp Leakey for more than forty years, was a cofounder of Orangutan Foundation International in 1986 (and is now its president), and is recognized as one of the world's leading experts on orangutans.

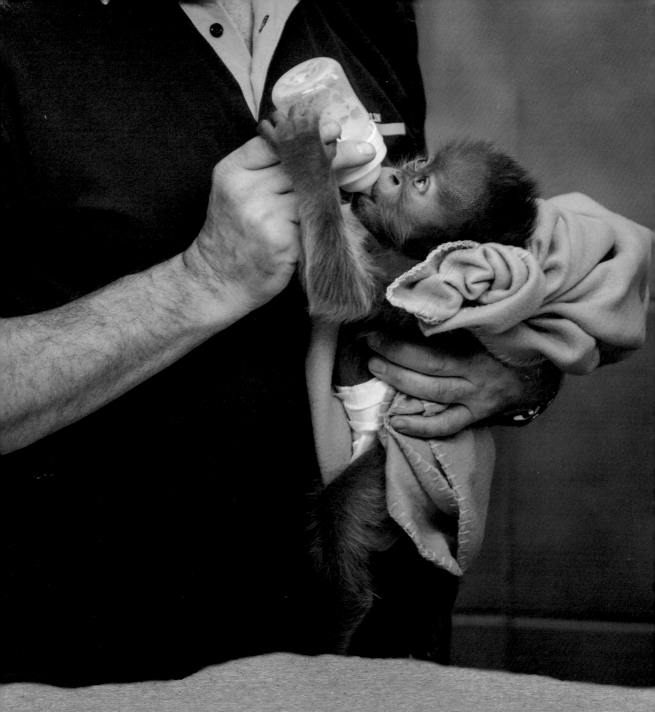

A zookeeper cares for a three-month-old orangutan. More than fifty zoos in North America participate in the Orangutan Species Survival Plan.

At Camp Leakey, Dr. Galdikas has not only conducted research but has also rehabilitated ex-captive and orphaned orangutans so that these great apes can be released back into the wild. Other orangutan rehabilitation centers include the Bohorok Orangutan Viewing Centre in Sumatra, the Wanariset Orangutan Rehabilitation and Reintroduction Center in Indonesian Borneo, and the Sepilok Orangutan Sanctuary in Malaysian Borneo.

When orangutans arrive at a rehab center, they live for a few weeks in quarantine isolated from the other orangutans. During these weeks of quarantine, rehab workers can ensure that the new orangutan does not pass diseases on to the other orangutans. The workers can also treat sick or injured animals.

Once an ape is released from quarantine, rehab workers begin teaching it how to be a wild orangutan. Mother orangutans spend seven or eight years teaching their babies to survive in the rain forest. Orangutans that have been raised as pets have not learned those survival skills. Rehab centers try to teach these orangutans how to climb trees, find food, and build nests. It can take several years to teach an orangutan how to survive in the wild. When the orangutan is ready, rehab workers will release it into the wild. Once the orangutan is released, it can still return to the rehab center for feedings. Rehab workers hope that a released orangutan will return to the center less and less over time until it finally becomes self-sufficient and no longer depends on the center for food.

PLEASE DO NOT
• Feed the Orangutans,
• Eat in front of the Orangutans, or
• Touch the Orangutans and

Please take your litter away with you
THANK YOU

Camp Leakey in Borneo started out as just two huts. It is now an established research facility.

Not all captive orangutans can become wild again, though. Some orangutans cannot learn the skills they need to survive because they have lived with people for too long and remain dependent on their human caregivers. These orangutans end up living in conservation centers for the rest of their lives. Expense is another concern. Rehabilitating orangutans is expensive. Caring for orangutans that cannot be rehabilitated is also expensive. Rehab centers often must scramble for funding.

Some conservationists believe rehabilitation could harm wild orangutan populations more than it helps them. They worry that captive orangutans will spread human diseases, such as tuberculosis and hepatitis, to orangutans in the wild. They also point out that some rehabilitated females never learn to be good mothers to their young.

But over the years, rehab centers have released more than eight hundred rehabilitated orangutans into the rain forest. Researchers have not found evidence that released orangutans have spread diseases or harmed the wild population.

## Saving the Orangutan

Until recently, experts believed about fifteen thousand to twenty-five thousand orangutans remained in the wild with five thousand to seven thousand in Sumatra and ten thousand to twenty thousand in Borneo. But in recent years, experts have realized that they had seriously underestimated the wild orangutan population.[1]

A tourist photographs a rehabilitated orangutan at Semenggoh Orangutan Rehabilitation Center near Borneo, Malaysia.

In 2002, Nature Conservancy researchers, led by scientist Scott Stanley, found a previously undiscovered population of orangutans in Eastern Borneo. Stanley estimates that two thousand orangutans live in this dense, swampy rain forest.

After forest fires devastated the rain forests of Borneo and Sumatra in the late 1990s, orangutan experts began new studies to find out how many orangutans had survived. In 2004, various wildlife groups combined their data. They found that there are about fifty thousand orangutans in the wild, which is nearly twice as many as they had previously thought.

In February 2013, conservation scientists conducted a field study of Bornean orangutans in Malaysia's Batang Ai National Park and Lanjak-Entimau Wildlife Sanctuary. They were encouraged to find leafy bedding high in the trees to nest up to two hundred of these rare primates. This new population offers more hope for the critically endangered red ape.

# Fast Fact!

Tigers are the orangutan's main predator. Other animals that will hunt this great ape are crocodiles, wild dogs, and clouded leopards.

# Chapter Notes

## Chapter 1. Great Apes of Asia

1. The IUCN Red List of Threatened Species, *Pongo Pygmaeus*, "Population," 2014, <http://www.iucnredlist.org/details/17975/0> (February 9, 2015).

2. Orangutan Foundation International. *Rainforest Facts*. 2014. <http://orangutan.org/rainforest/rainforest-facts> (February 9, 2015).

## Chapter 2. Meet the Orangutan

1. Gisela Kaplan and Lesley J. Rogers, *The Orangutans* (Cambridge, Mass.: Perseus Publishing, 2000), p. 22.

2. Stephen J. O'Brien, *Tears of the Cheetah* (New York: St. Martin's Press, 2003), pp. 128–129.

3. Ibid., p. 129.

4. Ibid., p. 130.

## Chapter 4. How Smart Are Orangutans?

1. Eugene Linden, *The Octopus and the Orangutan: More True Tales of Animal Intrigue, Intelligence, and Ingenuity* (New York: Dutton, 2002), p. 8.

2. Emily Sohn, "An Inspiring Home for Apes," *Science News for Kids*, July 14, 2004, <http:// student.societyforscience.org/article/inspiring-home-apes> (February 6, 2015).

## Chapter 5. A Look to the Future

1. NPR.org "Orangutan Metropolis Uncovered," November 20, 2002, <http://www.npr.org/templates/story/story.php?storyId=849785> (February 9, 2015).

# Glossary

**black market**—Buying and selling that is against government rules.

**captive**—Being confined or held in a safe place.

**conservation**—The protection of plants, animals, and natural resources.

**endangered**—In danger of becoming extinct and not existing on earth any more.

**extinction**—The death of an entire group or species of living things.

**frugivore**—An animal that feeds on fruit.

**gene**—A part of a cell that controls traits and characteristics, such as eye color, in a living thing.

**great ape**—A family of primates that includes gorillas, chimpanzees, and orangutans.

**palm oil**—A fat found in the fruit of some palm trees that is used in cooking and soap making.

**parasite**—An organism that lives in or on another organism to get protection or food.

**poacher**—A person who kills or steals wild animals illegally.

**population**—The total number of people, animals, or plants living in a specific area.

**species**—A group of animals or plants that have similar features. They can produce offspring of the same kind.

**tsunami**—A series of waves caused by a disturbance in the earth's crust in or near the ocean.

# Further Reading

## Books

Baillie, Marilyn, Jonathan Baillie, and Ellen Butcher. *How to Save a Species*. Toronto: Owlkids Books, 2014.

Charman, Andy. *I Wonder Why Dinosaurs Died Out and Other Questions About Extinct and Endangered Animals*. New York: Kingfisher, 2013.

Claus, Matteson. *Animals and Deforestation*. New York: Gareth Stevens, 2014.

Murray, Julie. *Orangutans*. Minneapolis, Minn.: ABDO, 2013.

Riehecky, Janet. *Orangutans*. North Mankato, Minn.: Capstone Press, 2013.

Yolen, Jane. *Animal Stories: Heartwarming True Tales from the Animal Kingdom*. Washington, D.C.: National Geographic Children's Books, 2014.

## Web Sites

**fws.gov/international/pdf/factsheet-great-ape.pdf**
*U.S. Fish & Wildlife Service's information about the Great Ape Conservation Fund*

**wcs.org/saving-wildlife/great-apes/orangutan.aspx**
*The Wildlife Conservation Society's facts about orangutans*

**worldwildlife.org/species/orangutan**
*A wealth of information on endangered orangutans*

# INDEX